THE AMAZING CHEMISTRY IN YOUR HOME

What are you reading?
A book about chemistry.
That sounds awful.
No way! Chemistry's amazing. Come see for yourself.

We're the brains of your mobile phone!

We're your brains— and your body too!

Watch out! You don't want to mess with us.

. . . but not me!

Leave us alone! We don't want to be friends with anyone.

								2 **He** Helium
			5 **B** Boron	6 **C** Carbon	7 **N** Nitrogen	8 **O** Oxygen	9 **F** Fluorine	10 **Ne** Neon
			13 **Al** Aluminum	14 **Si** Silicon	15 **P** Phosphorus	16 **S** Sulfur	17 **Cl** Chlorine	18 **Ar** Argon
28 **Ni** Nickel	29 **Cu** Copper	30 **Zn** Zinc	31 **Ga** Gallium	32 **Ge** Germanium	33 **As** Arsenic	34 **Se** Selenium	35 **Br** Bromine	36 **Kr** Krypton
46 **Pd** alladium	47 **Ag** Silver	48 **Cd** Cadmium	49 **In** Indium	50 **Sn** Tin	51 **Sb** Antimony	52 **Te** Tellurium	53 **I** Iodine	54 **Xe** Xenon
78 **Pt** latinum	79 **Au** Gold	80 **Hg** Mercury	81 **Tl** Thallium	82 **Pb** Lead	83 **Bi** Bismuth	84 **Po** Polonium	85 **At** Astatine	86 **Rn** Radon
110 **Ds** mstadtium	111 **Rg** Roentgenium	112 **Cn** Copernicium	113 **Nh** Nihonium	114 **Fl** Flerovium	115 **Mc** Moscovium	116 **Lv** Livermorium	117 **Ts** ennessine	118 **Og** Oganesson

We're the most expensive of all metals.

We can poison your whole life!

64 **Gd** adolinium	65 **Tb** Terbium	66 **Dy** Dysprosium	67 **Ho** Holmium	68 **Er** Erbium	69 **Tm** Thulium	70 **Yb** Ytterbium	71 **Lu** Lutetium
96 **Cm** Curium	97 **Bk** Berkelium	98 **Cf** Californium	99 **Es** Einsteinium	100 **Fm** Fermium	101 **Md** Mendelevium	102 **No** Nobelium	103 **Lr** Lawrencium

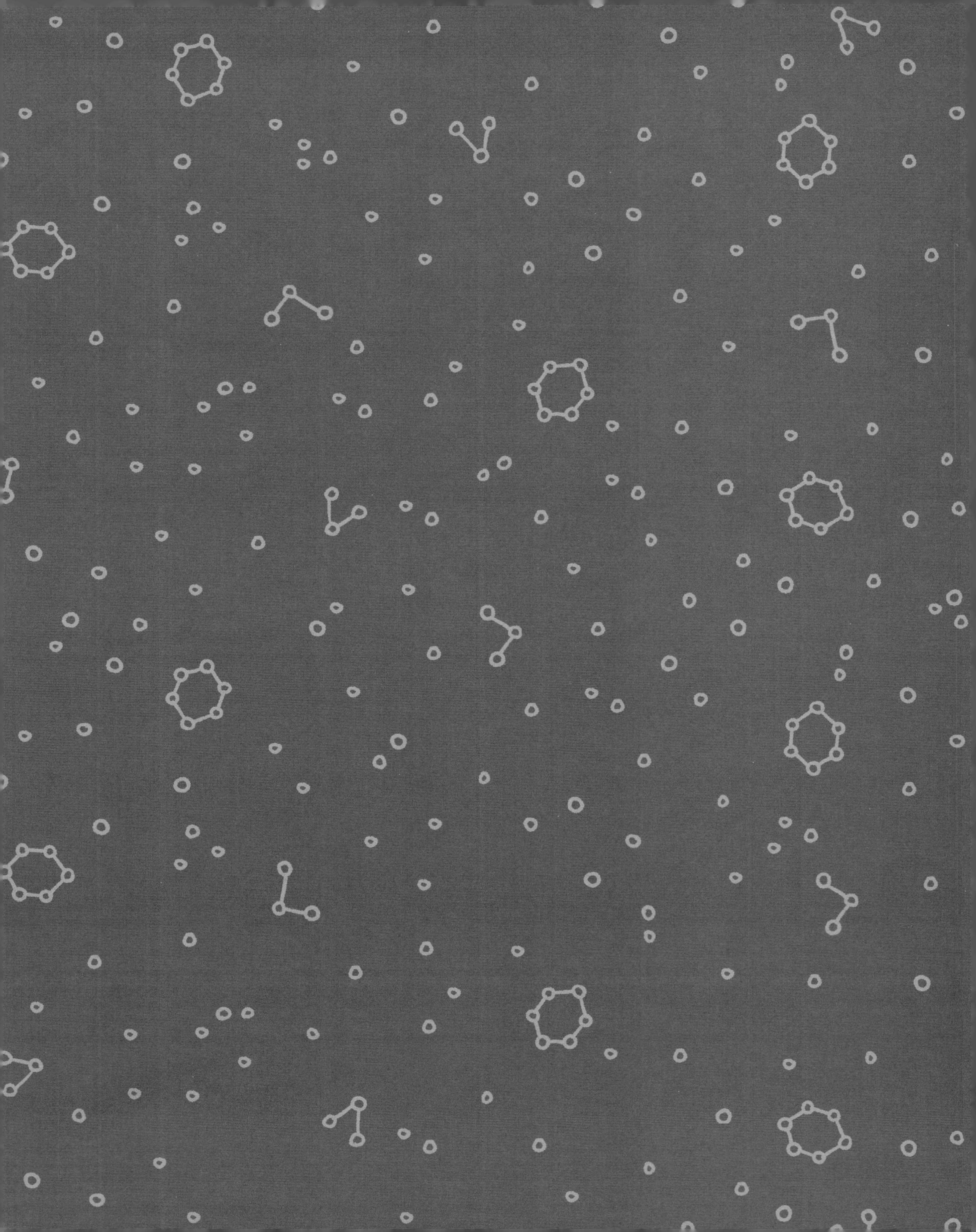

INTRODUCTION

What are elements?

Everything around us is made up of tiny particles called atoms. And inside them are even smaller particles: protons, neutrons, and electrons. When atoms have the same number of protons, we say they are the same chemical element. Elements are substances like gold, helium, oxygen, or uranium. Each element has its own chemical symbol—for example, Au for gold and He for helium.

nucleus of the helium atom

electrons around the nucleus

proton

neutron

All atoms look like blurry spheres. This one has two protons, so it's the element helium.

Why does the periodic table look like this?

If elements are arranged according to the number of protons, why is it not just a list from 1 to 118? Why do we need a table? Well, it's because there are electrons as well as protons in atoms. Elements look different and behave differently according to how many electrons they have and where these electrons live. Elements in the same column of the periodic table tend to look very similar and act similarly too. So we don't have to remember everything about each of the 118 elements; we just need to know about a few columns and rows.

What is the periodic table?

We know of 118 elements. To help people make sense of them, a scientist named Dmitri Mendeleev created the periodic table of elements in the 19th century. Back then, his table was a little emptier than it is today because lots of elements hadn't been discovered yet. But one thing has been the same since the beginning: elements are arranged in the periodic table according to how many protons they have (this is called the atomic number).

Everything suggests germanium should go here... I wish someone would hurry up and discover it!

Can all the elements be found in nature?

Some elements are not found in nature and have been artificially created by people in a lab. There are 24 of these in total, and all of them have 95 or more protons. These elements tend to be radioactive, which means they don't exist for long because they break down into other elements and particles.

AMAZING CHEMISTRY IN YOUR HOME

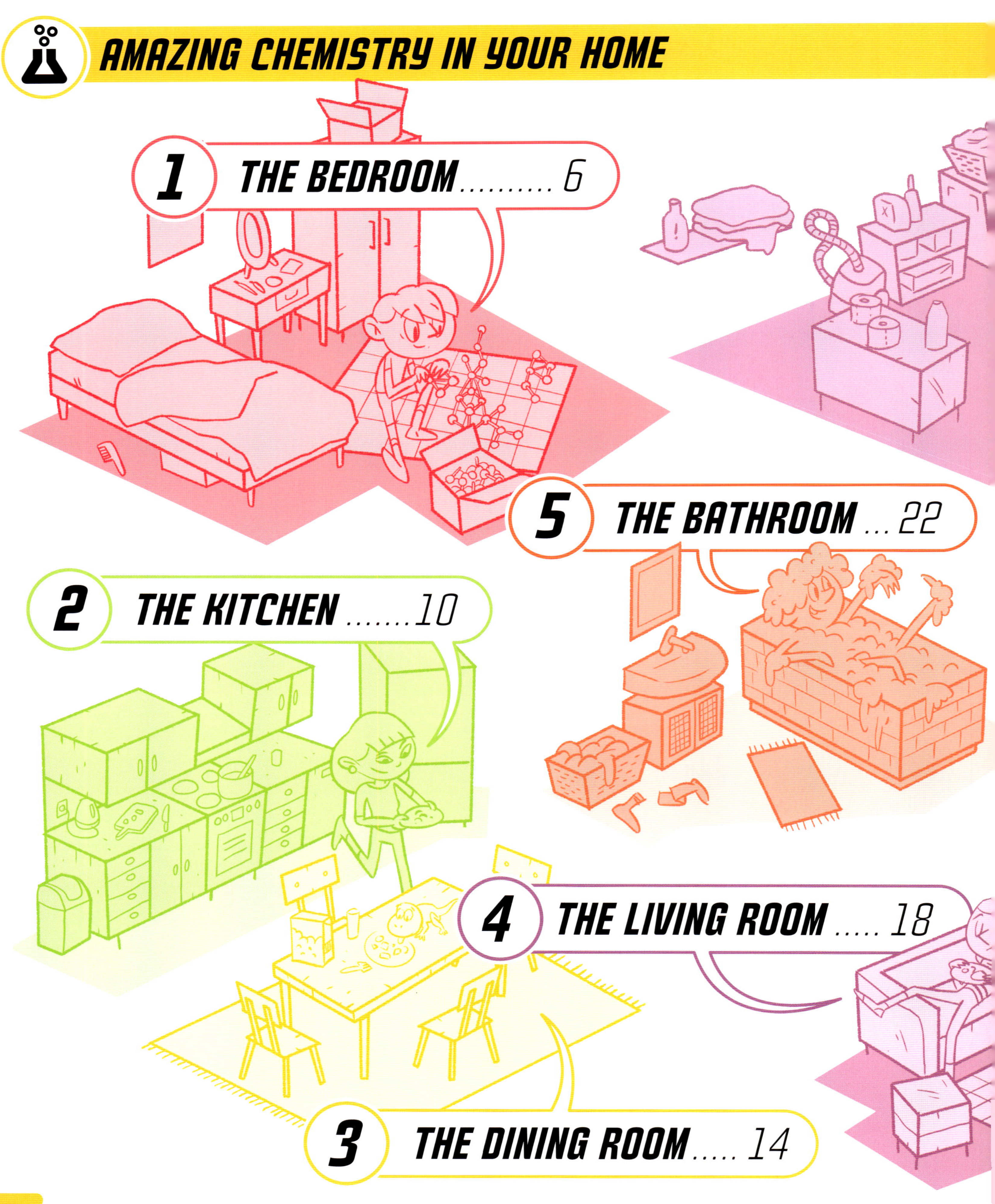

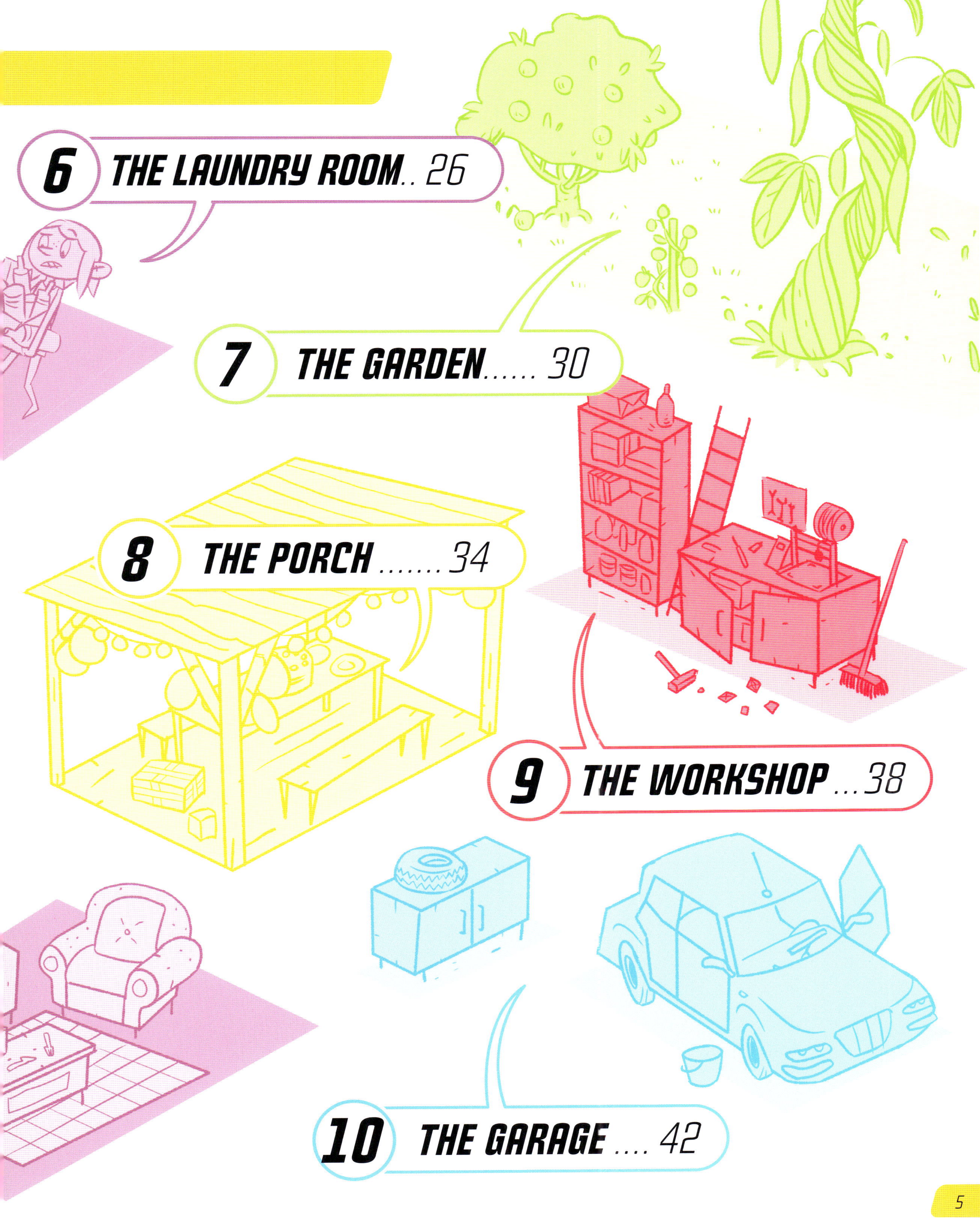

1 THE BEDROOM

Chemistry tells us what substances our world is made of and how they interact. Let's take a look at the individual building blocks—the chemical elements—that you can find in your room.

ATOMS AND MOLECULES

What is our world made of?

Look around you. Your favorite toy, your parents, this book—everything you can see and everything you can touch is made up of tiny particles called atoms. You definitely can't see them with the naked eye as they're about half a million times smaller than the thickness of one hair on your head.

Small and even smaller

Atoms are extremely small, but they're not the smallest thing we know of! The atoms themselves are made up of even smaller particles called electrons, protons, and neutrons. Electrons are like little flies that buzz around inside the atom. Protons are stable particles that sit with the neutrons in the nucleus at the center of the atom.

An atom's behavior depends on its number of protons. Hydrogen has 1 proton. Helium has 2 protons. These and other chemical elements are arranged on the periodic table in order of their number of protons—their atomic number—all the way up to 118.

Hydrogen belongs in water

Did you know that more than half of your body is water? This means you are mainly hydrogen and oxygen since those are the two elements that make up water. If a water molecule were a lot bigger, it would look like an oxygen head with two hydrogen arms.

A silicon brain

For your cell phone or tablet to be smart, it needs a brain. This is called a processor, and it can't work without silicon.

MATERIALS

Carbon chameleon

Just as doughnuts come in different flavors, carbon is found in lots of different forms. It's always the same carbon, but it can look different and act differently. Carbon can take the form of beautiful diamonds, of carbon fiber used to make expensive cars, or of the graphite in the lead of your pencil.

MATERIALS

GASES

Essential oxygen

With every breath of air, you inhale a mixture of elements. But only one is truly essential: oxygen! Life couldn't exist without it. And yet it only makes up about one-fifth of our air. The rest is made up mostly of nitrogen.

NATURE

What is the most common element on Earth?

Oxygen makes up almost half of all the atoms on Earth. This is followed by silicon, which makes up a quarter, and then aluminum. Together, these three elements account for more than 80% of the Earth's crust.

MATERIALS

Copper is the best

If copper is the best at anything, it's conducting electricity. That's why it's used in every cell phone to connect the processor to the battery, the camera, or even the buttons.

MATERIALS

The beauty of aluminum

Want to see what aluminum looks like? Take a look in the mirror! Mirrors all have a thin layer of aluminum that's really shiny, and that's why you can see yourself in them.

MATERIALS

Iron the strong

When you need something sturdy, iron will do the job. For example, chairs may have legs made of wrought iron so they can support your weight—or even a grown-up's.

MATERIALS

Attractive neodymium

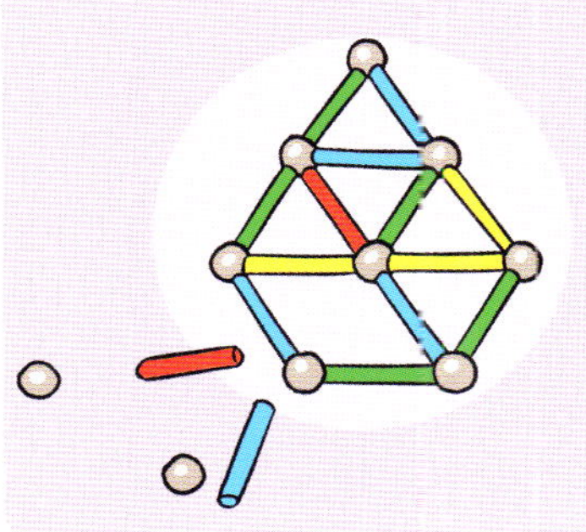

Powerful, silver-colored magnets are usually made of neodymium. They're absolutely great—unless your finger gets between two magnets flying toward each other. . . .

An atomic cocktail

Antsy atoms

Atoms are awfully fidgety. They're always moving about and wiggling and can't stay still for a second. You can see this when you're making tea. As the tea bag steeps, tea flows into the water all by itself. Thanks to the movement of atoms, you end up with a lovely cup of tea.

Even atoms need friends

Crash, bang, wallop! As atoms move around, it's only a matter of time before they collide. Sometimes they just rebound harmlessly off each other, but other times they stay together. Even atoms get lonely and want to find a companion, or even a few of them. They just have to meet the right atom, because not all elements can be friends. When atoms make friends, they grab each other's electrons as if they were holding hands, and then they become a molecule. A molecule looks and behaves totally differently from the individual atoms it's made up of. Molecules you might be familiar with include water, sugar, and the hydrochloric acid in your stomach.

chlorine and hydrogen combine to form hydrochloric acid

The water in the glass is still flowing nicely, and we call it a liquid.

Heat and cold

Imagine three glasses of water. You leave one on the table, put one in the freezer, and pour the last one into a kettle and switch it on. You'll see that the same chemical can behave very differently. It's found in different states depending on whether you heat it up or cool it down. And so every chemical can be a solid, a liquid, or a gas. Even oxygen can be a solid, though it would have to be cooled down to an extreme -362 °F. And even solid iron can become a gas, but it must be heated up to several thousand degrees Fahrenheit!

Chemical reactions

The friendship between atoms in molecules doesn't always last forever. Sometimes all it takes to break up the whole molecule is for another atom to come along. Or the molecule can make friends with another atom, making it bigger. When molecules form, fall apart, or change, we call this a chemical reaction. And these are happening everywhere, all the time. When you breathe or an apple ripens or a candle burns, those are all chemical reactions.

When molecules get hot

The higher their temperature, the faster and more active molecules become. Try making tea with cold water and hot water; you'll see that it brews a lot more slowly in cold water. We can put fast-moving, heated-up molecules to good use. As they're dashing about frantically they bump into other molecules more often—and that means more chemical reactions! The more you heat something up, the faster the reaction happens. For instance, if you turn the oven up, a cake will bake more quickly (and burn more quickly too).

Relighting a candle

One of the most common chemical reactions you'll come across is burning. You should never play with fire, but if your parent or another adult is around, they can safely show you some fun things about fire.

You will need

- **a responsible adult**
- **a candle**
- **matches**

Light the candle and let it burn for a while. Then carefully blow out the flame. A white plume of smoke will rise up from the wick. If you light this plume (not the wick), the fire will leap across to the candle and light it.

The white plume is evaporated wax that normally burns in the candle, and it can be relighted this way.

Only do this experiment under the supervision of a responsible adult!

2 THE KITCHEN

If there's one room that's full of tasty treats and sumptuous smells, it's the kitchen. There's a stove you can use to whip up a delicious meal, an oven with tempting scents wafting out of it, and the door to the secret, chilly world of the fridge, where you can always find something nice to eat—that is, unless it's past the expiration date!

HUMAN BODY

Why does our breath stink after eating garlic?

There's a reason people say hell stinks of sulfur: Wherever there's sulfur, there's usually a hellish stench. And it's the same with garlic. It has chemicals in it that contain sulfur, and that's what gives it such a strong smell. The problem is that it leaves the body mainly through the lungs, so your breath really stinks after eating garlic. If you have a big bowl of garlic soup—no matter how much you brush your teeth afterward—you won't get rid of that stinky breath.

MICROORGANISMS

Good and bad molds

Can I eat that moldy bread? You'd better not, unless you want to be sick. Some of the molds that grow on bread or tangerines can be poisonous, so it's best to throw out those kinds of spoiled food immediately. But not all molds are bad. Some are actually quite tasty—for example, the mold in Camembert or blue cheese. And some molds can even kill bacteria! It's thanks to them that we have antibiotics, which can be used to treat strep throat and other serious illnesses.

GASES

Cookers and cows

If you have a gas stove at home, it likely uses natural gas. Natural gas is mostly a flammable gas called methane. Funny enough, cows belch and fart out a lot of it. If someone came up with a way to capture cow farts, maybe we could cook with them!

Why does food go bad?

Bacteria are all around us. Some of them are good and help us digest food, while others are pests and can cause various illnesses. And some of them like to feast on our food. When they've eaten their fill, they leave behind chemicals that can be poisonous for our bodies. That's why we can get sick after eating spoiled food. Luckily, we have a weapon against bacteria: it's called the fridge. Bacteria don't do well in the cold, so food stays fresh longer in the fridge.

FOOD

Why do onions make us cry?

Onions are pesky vegetables! Whoever cuts into one starts crying. That's because when an onion is split, it sprays chemicals into the air that then transform into a new, even peskier chemical. When it gets into our eyes, it sets off an alarm, and we cry until all the nasty stuff is gone.

FOOD

The stink of rotten eggs

It's easy to tell if eggs are rotten: they would be incredibly stinky. It probably won't surprise anyone that sulfur has a hand in this. When eggs go bad, a chemical called hydrogen sulfide is produced, and it contains sulfur, which makes the eggs smell horrible.

GASES

Why does gas stink?

Natural gas smells pretty awful—but not on its own. That stink is added to it so that if there were a gas leak, we would at least be able to smell it if not see it. Can you guess which element makes gas smell? That's right, it's sulfur! It's also sulfur that makes the gases that come out of our bowels stink.

Time to chew the fat

It's sometimes said that fats are unhealthy, but that's not true! We need to eat fats. However, it's important not to overdo it and to choose the right ones. Some fats (like vegetable oils) are better for us, while others (like butter and lard) are less healthy. However, the worst of all are the hydrogenated oils found in processed foods.

The fat's in the fire!

What are hydrogenated fats (found in cookies, cakes, French fries, chips, and crackers) all about? They're fats that have been made solid. They start off as liquid vegetable oil, but then hydrogen is added, transforming them into solid fat. Although this kind of fat is cheap, tasty, and long-lasting, it's bad for your heart.

How come oil is a liquid but butter is a solid?

If fat were a lot bigger, it would look something like spaghetti. The fat in oils looks like strands of spaghetti sliding over each other. The fat in butter looks like spaghetti that's all tangled up. Outwardly, this tangled spaghetti acts like a solid piece of butter. But all you need to do is warm butter up a little—say, in your hands—and the spaghetti strands unravel and the butter melts.

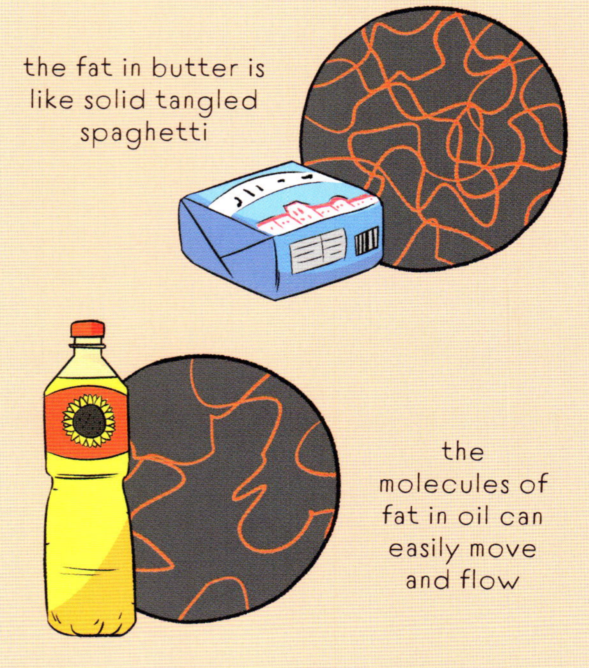

What's in margarine?

Instead of butter, you might spread margarine on your bread. This is a mixture of vegetable fats and water. Wait. . . what? You can't mix oil and water together! When you have soup, the oil floats on top, and no matter how much you stir, it will separate again and rise back to the top of the soup. That's where chemistry and chemicals called "emulsifiers" come in. They act as a kind of bridge that connects the water and fat so you end up with margarine.

fat
emulsifier
water

Margarine not only looks similar to butter; it also tastes like it. Once again, chemistry has a hand in this. A small amount of a chemical called diacetyl, which tastes and smells like butter, is added to margarine. But there's nothing wrong with it! It's the same substance that's found in butter.

Yum, I love diacetyl!

Chewing and digesting

Starch is to plants what belly fat is to us: a place to store energy reserves. But because plants don't have bellies, they store the energy as starch in seeds or tubers. So there's lots of starch in potatoes, rice, and grains—and that means it's in anything made of flour too.

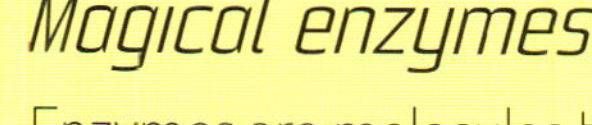

Magical enzymes

Enzymes are molecules that affect most of the processes in our bodies. For example, they help us digest food or fight off hostile germs.

Under a powerful microscope, starch looks like long chains with individual loops made up of sugars. When we eat starch, our bodies need to chop up this chain into individual sugar loops so that we can use the energy from it. Starch is cut up by molecules that help us with digestion. We call them enzymes, and we have them, for example, in our saliva.

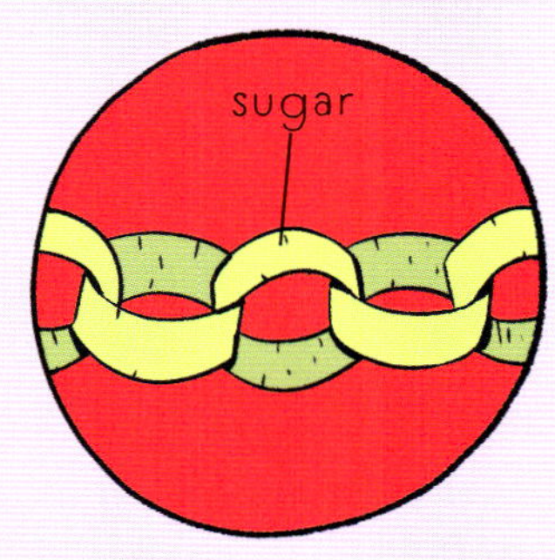

Sweet bread

You will need:

- bread
- a mouth
- saliva

Bite into a slice of bread and chew it for a long time. After a while it should get a bit sweeter. Bread is made from flour, which contains starch. When you chew bread, you mix it with saliva. Your saliva has enzymes in it that break down the starch into sugar, which is sweet.

3 THE DINING ROOM

Time for something nice to eat! The food's ready, and the house is filled with a delicious smell. All that's left to do is eat. But with what? And from what? Get your favorite spoon, bowl, and glass and come find out why they're much more interesting than it might seem!

MATERIALS

Polystyrene for lunch?

When you buy take-out food, there's a good chance it'll come in a disposable plastic container. These are usually made of foamed polystyrene, a white, airy foam that is also used to make cups, packaging for appliances, and home insulation. And just as polystyrene keeps heat inside a house, it also keeps your food warm.

MATERIALS

The Steel Age

When you want to eat food, it's usually better to use flatware. For instance, it's not that easy to eat soup with your hand, is it? The spoons, forks, and knives at home are likely made of stainless steel, which is mostly iron. However, iron on its own would rust the first time it was washed, and after several washes you wouldn't have anything to eat with. Iron and carbon are combined to create rust-resistant steel —so you don't have to buy a new set of flatware every week.

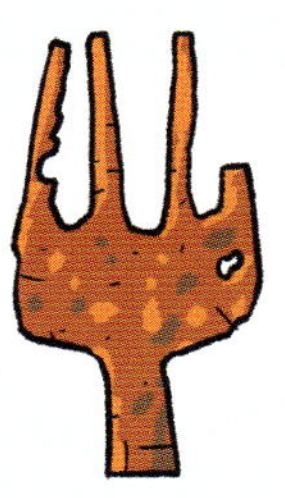

iron

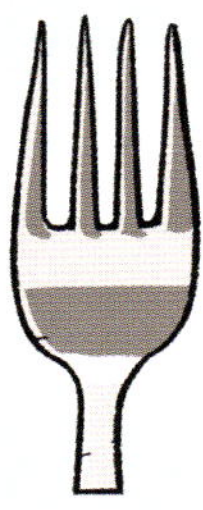

steel

MATERIALS

Corn cutlery

How do you make a spoon more environmentally friendly? By making it out of something natural! Disposable utensils are now being made from corn—or, more precisely, from polylactic acid (PLA for short), which is a hard plastic made from corn starch. And that's great because fewer chemicals are used to make it. But do you know what kind of cutlery is best? The metal kind that can be used over and over again.

plastic

PRODUCTION

Water in sand?!

No doubt you've got a favorite glass at home that you prefer to drink out of. And no doubt it's made of sand. Or rather, it used to be sand, or silica, which is the basis of all glass.

MATERIALS

Let's wrap it up

If your parents make you a snack for school, they might wrap it in tinfoil. This is silver-colored foil made from aluminum, the same material soda cans are made from. It's also used when roasting food because it can withstand very high temperatures.

MATERIALS

What to use on pans

Have you ever wondered why spatulas and spoons for cooking are usually made of plastic or wood? On the surface of some pans is a special coating that stops food from sticking to it. It's so thin that if you were to use metal utensils, it would get scratched off and the food would burn onto the pan more easily.

Flexible wood

Snacks can also be wrapped in transparent, flexible cellophane. This is made from cellulose, which is obtained from wood. So it's made from the same material as the paper of this book. Glycerine, which has a sweet taste, is also added to cellophane. That's why cellophane might seem sweet if you lick it.

Utensils, food's best friend

A king and his cabbage

If you want to dine the way kings did back in the olden days, get yourself some silver cutlery. But be aware that it's incredibly expensive and gets damaged quickly because silver is soft. It does have one advantage, though: silver can kill bacteria, so you'll have a lower chance of catching germs.

In the mid-20th century, cheap utensils made of pure aluminum were all the rage. At first it seemed like a good idea, but then it turned out that they started to dissolve if they came into contact with anything acidic. So anyone who ate sauerkraut from an aluminum dish using aluminum cutlery ended up eating a lot of unhealthy aluminum as well. That's why you shouldn't wrap sour snacks—even, say, an apple—in tinfoil.

What makes non-stick pans not stick?

What is non-stick coating? A chemist would say it's a polymer, meaning that it's made up of lots of little molecules linked together into one big network. This polymer contains lots of carbon and fluorine atoms. They like being together and hold on to each other so tightly they don't let anyone else in. Not even food can latch onto them. Non-stick coating is used to make not only pots and pans but also for sealing and piping.

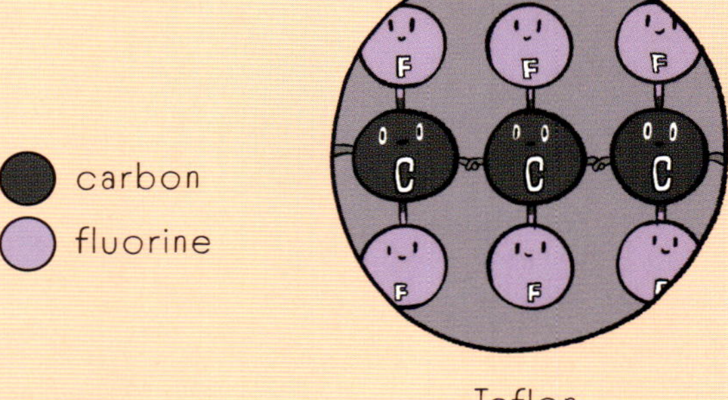

Teflon

The non-stick gecko

Do you know how to confuse a gecko? Put it in a non-stick frying pan (but don't put it on the stove!). Geckos have amazingly sticky toes that allow them to climb up anything—well almost anything. A non-stick pan is so non-sticky that geckos slide over it the way we do when wearing boots on ice.

The non-stick sticky wicket

Never leave a pan unattended on a hot stove! Not only can you burn the house down, but when a non-stick pan heats up to a very high temperature, it begins to break down, releasing toxins into the air. The resulting fumes can be harmful to pets—especially birds—as well as people.

How to make glass

First you need some sand and other substances to color the glass or improve it in other ways. All of the ingredients are put in a furnace, where they are melted at very high temperatures—even as high as 3632°F. This produces molten glass, which is poured into a mold, left to cool, and ta-da! The glass is ready!

And how can we improve the glass? If we want the glass to withstand high temperatures without cracking, then we add the element boron. This produces borosilicate glass, which is used to make things like oven dishes, test tubes, flasks, and beakers.

a glass furnace with molten glass

Although most metals are silver-colored, when they're mixed into glass, they can produce all the colors of the rainbow. You need iron for green glass, manganese for purple, cobalt for blue, and gold for red glass. In the past, radioactive uranium was also used to color glass, giving it a beautiful green glow. Unsurprisingly, considering how toxic uranium is, no one wants to drink out of those glasses anymore. . . .

Where do bowls come from?

Some bowls, plates, and cups are made of porcelain. But this isn't a modern material: the first porcelain dishes were made in China more than 2,000 years ago! If you want to make a porcelain dish, you need to get hold of a special rock: kaolin. Form it into a ceramic clay and shape the bowl. Then find someone with a really hot kiln to fire the bowl for you. At high temperatures, the clay starts to transform and the molecules in it join together into a giant, solid network. Then the finished porcelain bowl is taken out of the kiln—just be sure not to drop it!

4 THE LIVING ROOM

REACTIONS

Fizzy tablets

Fizzy tablets are fantastic. You toss one in some water, and it transforms into flavored, bubbly water. For fizzy tablets to fizz, they have to contain two things: citric acid and baking soda. These two powders are compressed together into a tablet. Until they come into contact with water, nothing happens. But as soon as the tablet touches water, the citric acid and baking soda dissolve and begin to react with each other and fizz. This produces carbon dioxide, filling the water with bubbles.

You can do all kinds of things in the living room—for example, have breakfast with your family or friends. But why is it that breakfast tastes so good? Where do those soft doughnuts come from, or the sweet honey we put in tea? Quick, get up! Come have something to eat!

* This is really doughy.

GASES

Bubbly bread

Fresh homemade bread can be soft and fluffy—thanks to carbon dioxide. It's a gas that's produced in the dough during kneading or baking. Its bubbles make bread rolls bigger and fluffier. But how does it get into the bread in the first place?

Made either from yeast . . .

Yeasts are microorganisms that are added to dough. They eat sugar and turn it into carbon dioxide, which puffs up the dough. But it takes a while, which is why you have to allow time for yeast dough to rise.

. . . or from baking soda

Baking soda, or bicarbonate of soda, reacts with acids like yogurt or molasses to produce carbon dioxide—the reaction starts immediately so get it into the oven fast! For recipes that don't include something acidic use baking powder instead, which just needs liquid to create bubbles. Both make cakes light and airy.

Don't eat that sugar. You'll start passing gas again!

Colored eggs

Eggs are popular at breakfast time. But why are eggs sometimes brown and sometimes white? It depends on many factors, but mainly on the breed of the hen. A white leghorn lays white eggs and a Rhode Island Red lays brown eggs. And you can often predict the egg color from the color of the hen's earlobes! There are even hens that can lay green or blue eggs. They get their color from the same pigment that's in bruises. Fascinating, right?

NATURE

Caff-what?

A hot drink with breakfast warms us up. Grown-ups often choose tea or coffee because they contain caffeine, which helps them feel awake and alert. But caffeine is a bit of a trickster—it makes the brain think it's not tired, even when it is. Once it wears off, you can suddenly feel really sleepy! That's why coffee isn't suitable for kids. Your body and brain need real rest, not a caffeine cover-up. So stick to water, milk, or juice—your brain will thank you later!

HUMAN BODY

Sweet and sticky

They say life should be sweet. And if you want to sweeten your tea at breakfast time, honey is a great choice. Bees make honey from the sweet nectar of plants. They take the nectar back to the hive, where other bees repeatedly drink it and then bring it back up again. This gets the nectar nice and thick. As soon as the bees are happy with the result, they pack the thickened nectar into a honeycomb and start flapping their wings at it so that as much water as possible evaporates. This creates a thick mass full of sugar, which is actually sweet, delicious honey. Who'd have thought something so wonderful has passed through so many stomachs?

The interesting thing about honey is it never goes bad. If any nasty bacteria were to get into it, they simply wouldn't survive. That's because honey has so much sugar that it would suck all the water out of the bacteria. On top of that, honey contains chemicals from the bees' stomachs, such as hydrogen peroxide, which would cause those germs a lot of trouble.

NATURE

What are you having for breakfast?

PRODUCTION

Not all teas are alike

What kind of tea will you have: black, green, or fruit tea? And what kind of fruit: strawberry, cherry, or perhaps berry? There are so many to choose from! But what's the difference between them all?

FRUIT TEA
doesn't contain any tea leaves. It's full of dried fruit, berries, and herbs. That means it has no caffeine in it and can be drunk by anyone, anytime.

GREEN AND BLACK TEA
start off as the green leaves of the tea plant, but whether they will turn into green or black tea depends on what people do with them.

FOOD

The egg

An egg has a shell to make it strong and tough—well, at least a little bit. Eggshells are made up of tiny crystals of calcium carbonate. This is found in nature as limestone, and it can form whole mountain ranges. It was also used to make the Great Sphinx of Giza, which has been standing for a few thousand years, so we have proof that limestone can withstand a lot—unless you drop the egg, that is. But now let's look at the parts of the egg that taste a lot better.

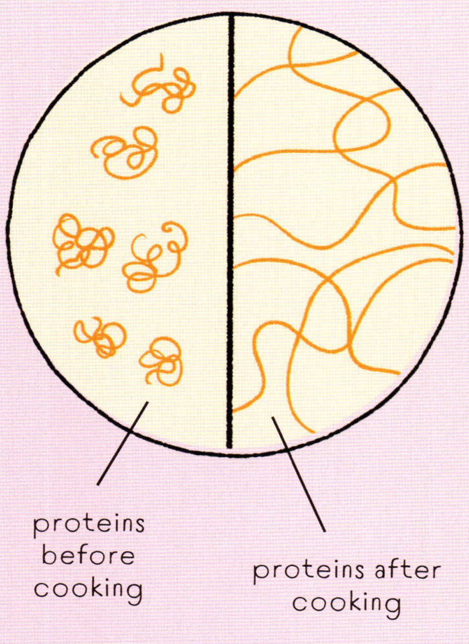

Egg whites are runny and translucent, but if you heat them up properly, they'll become solid, white, and delicious. But why do they change color when they're cooked? It's because egg whites contain a lot of proteins, which start to transform when heated, gradually forming a stiff network. This is called denaturation, and it happens at a lower temperature in the white than in the yolk. This means that your breakfast egg can have a solid white and a nice, soft yolk at the same time.

Eggs are one of the few foods that contain vitamin D. This vitamin gives us strong bones, and it's normally produced by our bodies when we're out in the sun. So if you're a vampire, we recommend eating eggs for breakfast!

green tea

GREEN TEA
is quite simple to make: fresh tea leaves are gently heated so they stay green. Then they're dried and crushed. Each part of the world has its own way of making tea, which is why you'll find so many different packets in shops.

black tea

BLACK TEA
is made in a different way: the tea leaves are left to air-dry till they turn brown. It's like when an old banana goes brown through a process called oxidization. Then the leaves are dried, so they get even darker, which is why we call this tea black.

Metal cereals

You can also start the day with cereal and milk or yogurt. These foods can be full of healthy nutrients such as protein, fiber, and vitamins, as well as unhealthy ones—in particular, lots of sugar. But you can also find substances that you might not expect, such as iron. What's it doing there? We're not robots who need to eat iron, are we?

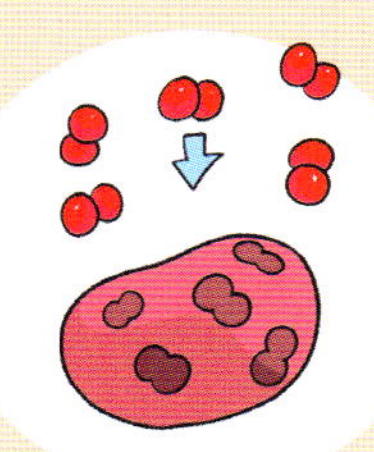

oxygen binds to a red blood cell in the lungs

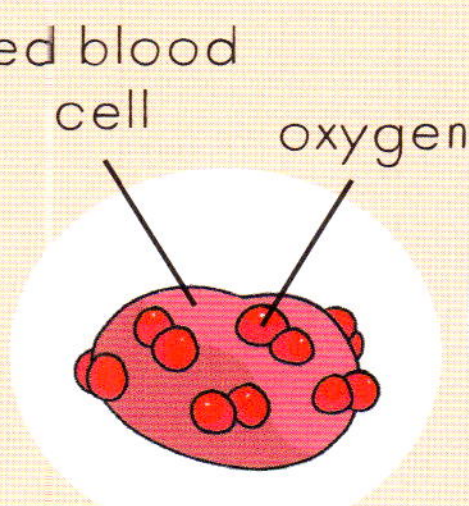

blood cell carries oxygen around the body

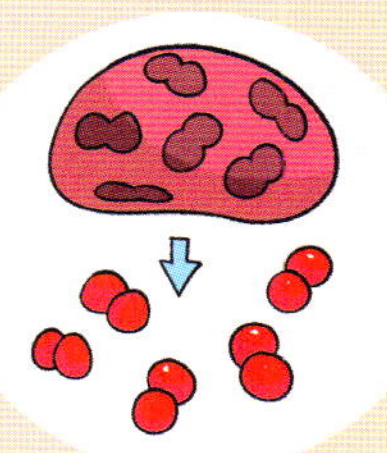

blood cell releases the oxygen in the right place

Well, yes and no. We're not robots, but humans—and especially our blood—need iron too. In blood, there are lots and lots of red blood cells. These red blood cells capture the oxygen in the lungs and deliver it to the rest of the body. Red blood cells contain a lot of a substance called hemoglobin, which contains iron. If people don't have enough iron, they don't get enough oxygen, and then they feel really tired.

Cereal iron

You can find iron in meat and beans, but it is also added to cereal. What does it look like then?

You will need:

- cereal containing iron, ideally with no chocolate
- a powerful magnet
- a plastic bottle with water
- a plastic bag

First, crush a handful of cereal into small pieces—preferably in a plastic bag—and then pour them into a plastic bottle about a third of the way full of water. Put the top on the bottle, give it a good shake for at least two minutes, and let it sit for about half an hour. Then, take the magnet, hold it against the bottle, near the cereal, and slowly turn the bottle so the magnet attracts as much iron as possible. Slowly lay the bottle on its side, and you'll see that little bits of iron filings have been picked up by the magnet. This is exactly the form iron takes in cereal. Although it may look a little strange at first, our bodies can easily process these iron filings to top off the iron in our bodies.

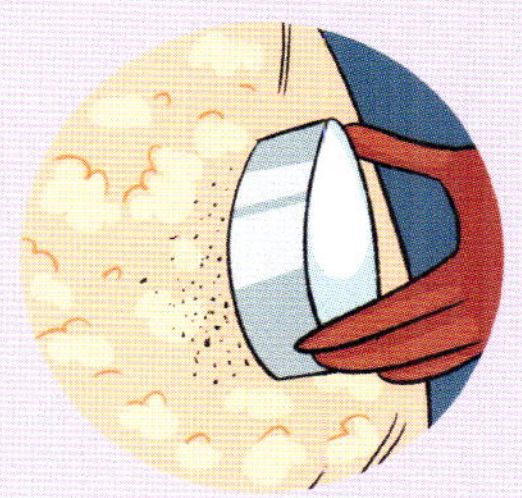

5 THE BATHROOM

The bathroom is a magical place. People go into it dirty and emerge a little while later transformed, clean and fragrant. How are these magic tricks really done?

Rainbow nails

When someone paints their nails, it can smell pretty strong. Nail polish contains a solvent that evaporates, leaving a layer of colored varnish on the nails. When you want to remove varnish from nails, you can't do it with water or soap. It needs a similarly stinky solvent—for example, acetone.

I want to have extra-clean teeth today!

Dissolve, dirt!

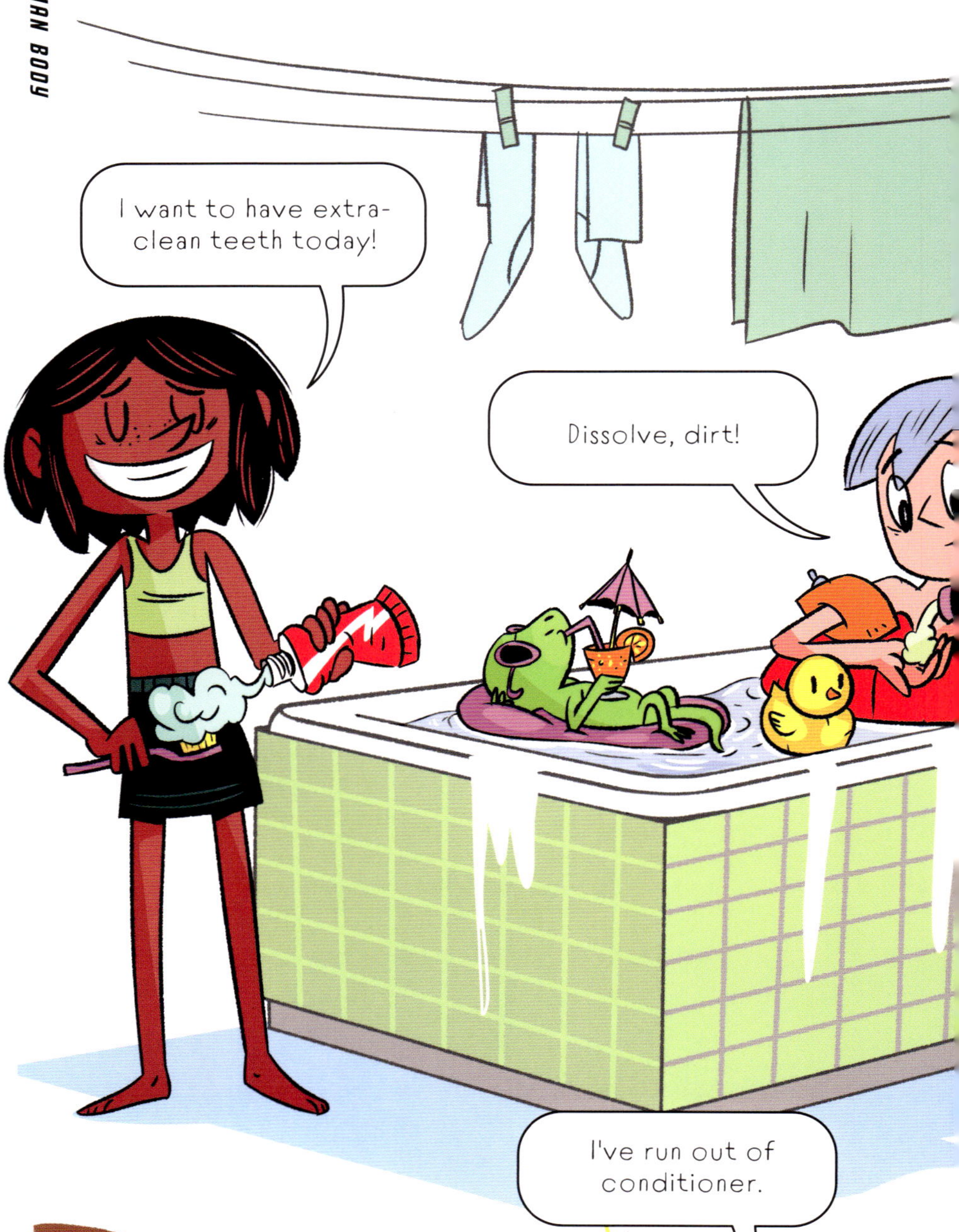

To sweat or not to sweat?

Sometimes we run somewhere and work up a real sweat—especially under the arms, where various bacteria feast on our perspiration. And then it starts to get pretty stinky under there. To keep BO at bay, we can use underarm deodorant, which masks the smell. Or we can stop the sweating using antiperspirant. Like deodorant, this makes us smell nice, but it also blocks the pores in our skin so the sweat can't get out. The effect is only temporary, though: in time, the pores clear and we start to sweat again.

I've run out of conditioner.

A condition for beautiful hair

If you have long hair, after washing it, you probably reach for the conditioner. That's because shampoo strips your hair of oils. Without them, your hair is dry, dull, and lifeless. Dry hair is also more prone to static electricity, so when you brush it, it sticks out in every direction. But conditioner coats hair in a thin layer that prevents all these ailments.

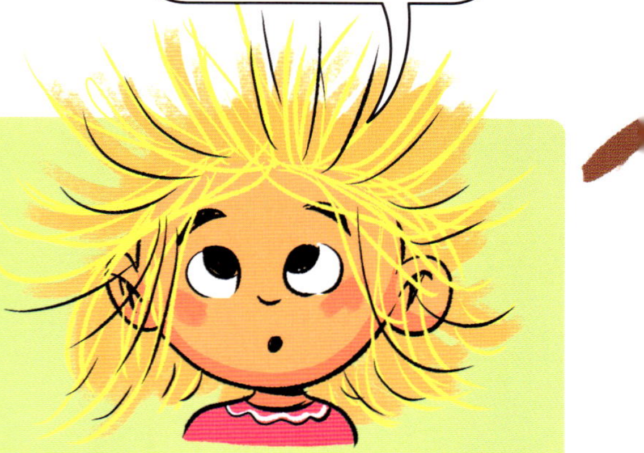

A soggy lifesaver

When a baby's wearing a diaper, it's best for everyone if nothing spills out and everything stays inside. That's why there's a layer of material in a diaper we call a superabsorbent polymer. This is able to absorb a huge amount of urine; it turns solid and doesn't leak out, and the whole diaper can be thrown away.

How much water can a superabsorbent polymer soak up?

A people-cleaner

If you look at soap under a really powerful microscope, it looks a little like worms. They've got a head at one end and a tail at the other. When there's dirt on something that can't be washed off with water, soap worms come to the rescue! They stick their tails in the dirt and bite into the water with their heads. By doing this, the worms connect the dirt to the water, making it easy to wash off.

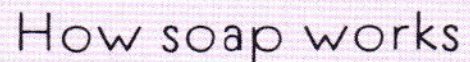

How soap works

How is soap made?

Soap isn't exactly a new invention—the ancient Babylonians figured out it was good to be clean and smell nice. It wasn't hard to make soap: you just had to get hold of some fat and ash and boil them together. The interesting thing is that the production of soap hasn't changed that much in 5,000 years. These days, fats are boiled with soda, a chemical that's found in ash. There's a good chance your soap was once a cow, since beef fat is most often used.

Why are these things in my shampoo?

Shampoo is a real cocktail of substances. Which ones are the most important?

So there's plenty of it

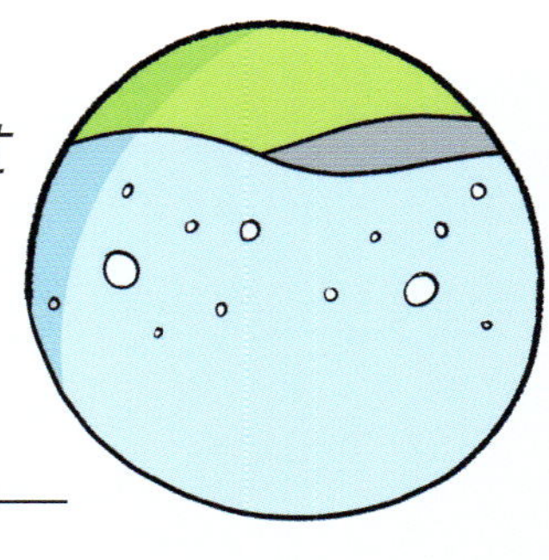

Shampoo is mainly water, so nearly everything dissolves in it.

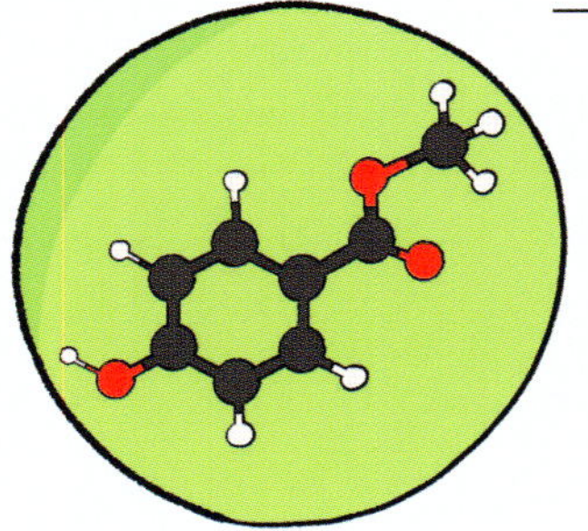

So it lasts a long time

Parabens stop shampoo from going bad. But some people are allergic to them and leave the bathroom with not just clean hair but also a rash! That's why these chemicals are gradually being replaced by other ones.

So your hair is clean

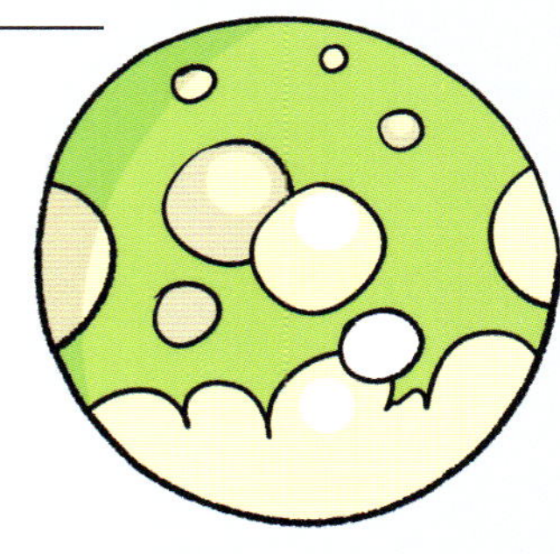

Shampoo's cleaning power mostly comes from "surfactants," chemicals that can dissolve dirt, allowing it to disappear with the water down the drain.

So it flows slowly

Salt is also added to shampoo (but don't test it with your tongue). When salt comes into contact with surfactants, they turn into a thick, slow-pouring liquid, allowing you to pour the shampoo into your hand and not straight down the drain.

So you have shiny hair

Silicone makes your hair soft and shiny. The best kinds are easy to wash off, as some can stick tightly to hair. Because of silicone, hair dries out over time and can break more easily.

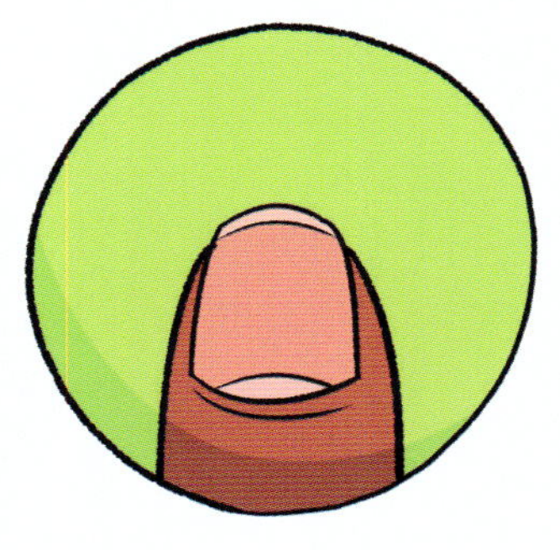

So you have strong hair

Natural extracts such as keratin are often added to shampoo. Keratin is what our hair and nails are made of. Shampoo tops off the keratin in hair, making it stronger.

Why are these things in my toothpaste?

Brushing teeth isn't rocket science, but we'll get to the root of the matter!

So it flows

Half of ordinary toothpaste is made up of water.

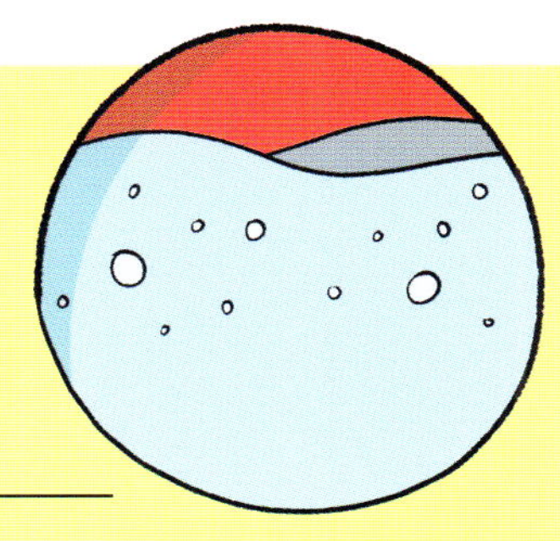

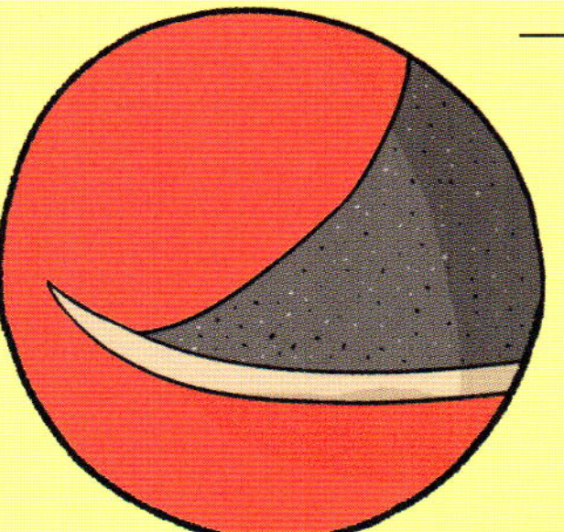

So your teeth stay white

This is the most important thing in toothpaste: small, rough particles that scrub the dirt off your teeth, making them a bit whiter. They turn toothpaste into a kind of liquid sandpaper.

So your teeth don't rot

Whether it's from food or soft drinks, we usually have some acids in our mouth. These can eat away at our teeth, making it easier for them to decay. To make sure this doesn't happen baking soda is added to toothpaste to destroy the acids in our mouth so we can smile with confidence.

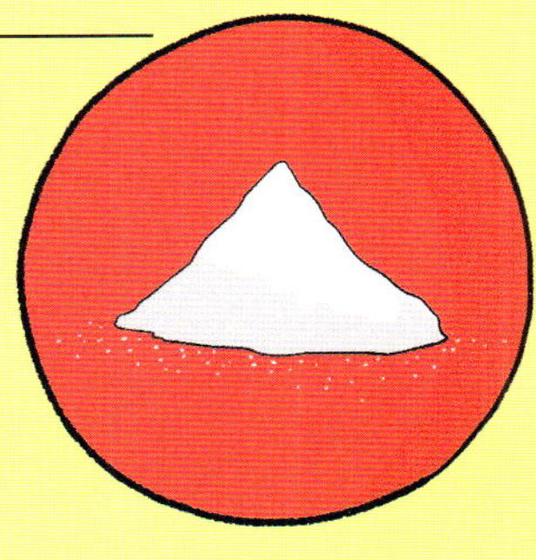

So it foams up

Sulfates clean teeth and lather up the toothpaste. But there's a catch: they mess with our sense of taste. For a while after brushing our teeth, we taste sweet things less and bitter things more. So if you have something like orange juice after toothpaste, you'll notice it tastes really horrible.

So our teeth grow stronger

On the surface of our teeth is enamel, which is very tough. To make it even stronger, a chemical called fluoride is added to toothpaste. This packs itself into the enamel, transforming it into a tougher material that even acids have trouble breaking down.

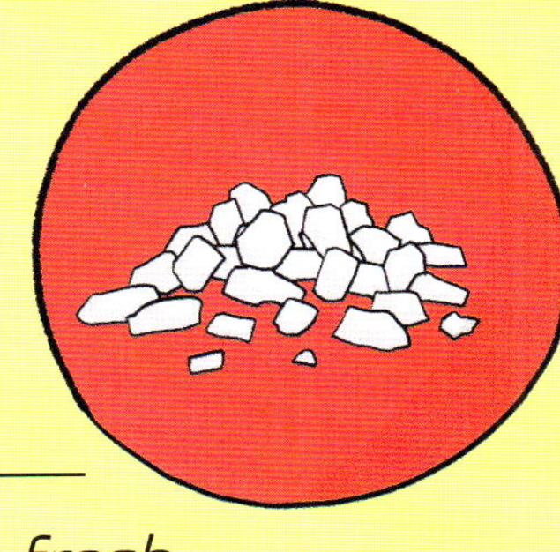

So our breath is fresh

To freshen our breath, menthol is added to toothpaste. It's a chemical that's found in mint. But menthol can also fool us. It latches on to areas in your mouth whose job it is to sense cold. So we think our mouth is cold, but it's really just an illusion.

6 THE LAUNDRY ROOM

It's always nicer when the house is clean. But keeping a big house in order takes a lot of effort, hard work, and the right chemicals!

REACTIONS

Why does bleach bleach?

Bleach is a real troublemaker. As soon as it sees a pigment, bleach pounces and chews it to bits, removing the original color. For instance, it'll turn a black T-shirt into a brown or even white one. But its bleaching abilities aren't always bad for clothes: bleach is deliberately added to white laundry to make it even whiter.

MATERIALS

Paper all around

Do you know what toilet paper, napkins, tissues, cotton balls, cotton swabs, and normal paper have in common? They're all made from the same material: cellulose. People get it from trees and plants, so everything that's made from cellulose can easily break down in nature. Isn't that great?

REACTIONS

The more the scarier

If you wanted to make cleaning easier, you might think, "Let's mix all the cleaning products together!" But that's a very bad idea—don't ever do it! The chemicals in cleaning products are really aggressive and eager to attack dirt. If two of these chemicals come into contact, they will even attack one another. This can result in new, even nastier chemicals, which get into the air and poison anyone who breathes them in.

What is limescale?

There are lots of minerals dissolved in water that can collect on pipes or appliances as the water is heated and evaporates. They turn into something called limescale, which can appear as a white or even brown layer in a kettle or marks on a tap. Limescale on a tap may look horrible, but inside a washing machine, it can do real damage. A broken washing machine won't clean your clothes, so it's important to get rid of limescale every once in a while.

MATERIALS

Why wash in warm water?

We usually wash dishes and clothes in warm water. If you're cleaning by hand, the warmth obviously makes it more pleasant. But washing machines know what they're doing too. Warm water washes better because dirt dissolves better in it. And warm water has another trick up its sleeve: it can squeeze into nooks and crannies more easily, so it reaches the dirt better than cold water does.

TEMPERATURE

A sweet problem

You will need:

- two cups or glasses
- two spoons
- cold and hot water
- granulated sugar

Pour cold water into one of the cups or glasses and hot water into the other. It's probably best to ask a grown-up for help with the hot water. Put five tablespoons of sugar in each cup and stir it well for a while. In which cup did the sugar dissolve more? The sugar dissolved more in the hot water because sugar dissolves more easily in hot water than in cold water. In time, the sugar would dissolve in the cold water as well, but it would take longer. It's the same with dirt: it dissolves a lot faster in hot water.

What a mess!

There's a solution to every problem—and a cleaning product for every type of dirt.

1 A blocked sink

Sinks and bathtubs have a tough job. Food scraps, dirt, and hair often end up in the drain and clog the pipes. To clear a clog, some people use lye, also known as caustic soda—one of the strongest household chemicals. It eats through grime but can also burn your skin. A safer option is a plunger, also called a "plumber's helper," to push the clog through, or a snake—a long, skinny tool used to pull blockages out of the drain.

2 Mold

Molds are fungi that can look like black spots or even greenish-white clumps. They thrive in warm, damp places, so they absolutely adore bathrooms. The nasty thing about molds is that they release spores, and if there are a lot of them, people find it hard to breathe. So it's best to crack down on mold. Bleach can work on some surfaces, but the best thing to do is to get rid of the moisture problem, or the mold will just grow back.

!

The main chemical in bleach is sodium hypochlorite. Hypochlorite attacks mold, bacteria, pigments, your skin . . . basically anything it comes across. It produces stinky chemicals that are good to air out, so you might want to open a window.

Paper towels

Not all paper is soft and white. Some paper towels are brown and feel a bit rough—definitely not something you'd want as toilet paper! That's because they've been paper before. They're made from recycled paper: shredded, boiled, cleaned, and turned into new paper. It might not look fancy, but it helps save trees. So next time you see a brown paper towel, you'll know it's doing a good job for the planet—even if it feels like it could sand wood!

3 The electric kettle

Acids like vinegar or lemon juice dissolve limescale, which is mostly calcium carbonate. The acid reacts with the calcium carbonate, creating new substances—one of them is carbon dioxide gas, which makes bubbles! That's why acidic ingredients such as acetic or citric acid are used in cleaning products to remove limescale from kettles and taps.

Chemistry to the rescue!

4 Dishes

Detergents are used for greasy things like dishes. They're the superheroes of the soap world! That's because they contain surfactants—special molecules that grab onto both water and grease, helping them mix. This breaks up the grease so it can be washed away.

Ouch! Someone's been cleaning. . . .

5 The window

The most important thing when cleaning windows is that there are no smudges left on them! That's why glass cleaners contain a lot of alcohol, which quickly evaporates so you can see in the mirror without any smears.

Nothing but cellulose

Both absorbent cotton and paper are made mostly of cellulose, but what's the difference between them? Each comes from a different source! Absorbent cotton is made from cotton, the downy white tufts on the flowers of the cotton plant. Paper, on the other hand, is made from trees, potatoes, and rocks. Seriously! Cellulose comes from wood, which is ground up, boiled in chemicals, and pressed. Starch (for instance, from potatoes) is added to the paper to make it stronger and limestone to make it less see-through.

7 THE GARDEN

In a garden, there may be lots of plants that will someday produce sweet tomatoes, delicious potatoes, or crunchy carrots. Before that happens, they need a lot of tender, loving care. But what do they actually want?

NATURE

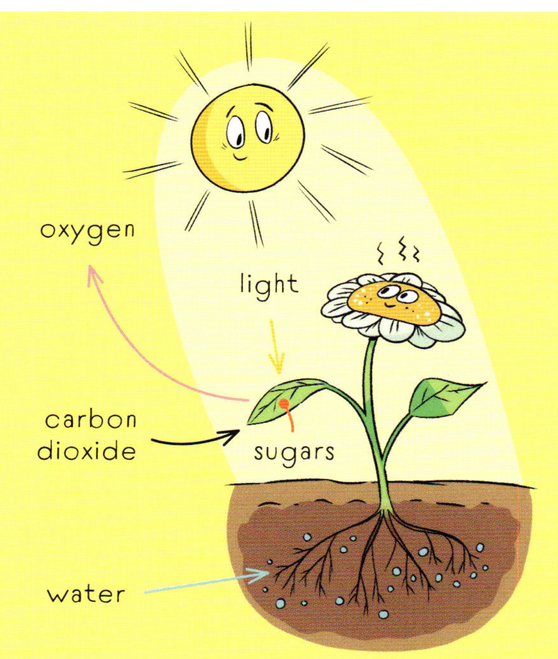

What do plants have for breakfast?

When the sun comes up in the morning, plants can start their breakfast. That's because plants use sunlight to make oxygen and sugars out of water and carbon dioxide. And that's how plants get their energy. But a happy plant needs much more than that, just as people wouldn't be healthy if they only ate sugar.

NATURE

What else do plants need?

Lots of minerals! To make sure there are plenty of them, fertilizers are added to the soil. They usually contain three elements: nitrogen, phosphorus, and potassium. These fertilizers are called NPK after the chemical symbols for these elements. Another good fertilizer is guano—aka bird or bat droppings. In the old days, mountains of bird droppings were mined for this purpose!

Where to get fertilizer

The more people there are in the world, the more food we need to grow, and that takes a lot of fertilizer. But what to make it from? Well, from air! We've got no shortage of air, right? And it's nearly all nitrogen, a real feast for flowers. It just needs to be prepared in such a way that plants can absorb it. That's why airborne nitrogen is used to make ammonia, a really smelly chemical, which is then turned into a kind of fertilizer called nitrate. This made life so much easier for people that the man who invented the method for producing ammonia, Fritz Haber, was awarded a Nobel prize!

The water's blooming

Plants in gardens and fields thrive when they get a good dose of fertilizer. But there's a catch. When it rains, the water washes the fertilizer into rivers, ponds, and lakes. This nutrient-rich water is a paradise for cyanobacteria, green bacteria that grow and grow until the whole pond is green. And it's poisonous for fish and other animals. If you go for a dip in this green water, you'll probably come out red, as it can give you a nasty rash. . . .

How did they do it in the Middle Ages?

Nowadays you can buy fertilizer in any shop, but it wasn't always like that. Getting fertilizer used to be hard, smelly work. First you had to find lots of excrement—the more the better. It didn't matter if it came from an animal or human. Then you piled it up, poured urine over it, and after a year or so, crystals of an excellent fertilizer called nitrate would form on it. Then you had to pluck up the courage to go and collect them. It's a good thing this smelly job is a thing of the past. . . .

A pretty toxic garden!

Poison grows on trees

Apples, apricots, peaches, plums . . . Who'd have thought such delicious fruit could be dangerous?! But all these fruits contain amygdalin, which is poisonous. Luckily, it's only found in the seeds, so as long as you don't eat the pits along with the fruit, nothing will happen to you. Amygdalin is also found in other tasty treats, like almonds. There are different types of almonds, and the nice, sweet ones we normally eat are low in amygdalin. However, there are also bitter almonds that have so much amygdalin that ten of them would be enough to poison you.

How many fruits with cores or pits would it take to poison a person?

67

apples

25

apricots

13

plums

12

peaches

Deadly tomatoes?

Tomatoes first grew in South America, and it took a while before the rest of the world found out about them. They were a hit in 19th-century Europe, because that was when the modern pizza was invented in Italy and people fell in love with tomatoes. But in England and the US, people were scared of bright, red tomatoes, which is usually a warning sign in nature, and because the plants are related to the very poisonous belladonna. At first, people grew them as decorative plants and only later plucked up the courage to eat them.

Don't eat green potatoes

When a potato is growing, sometimes part of it will peek out of the ground into the sunshine. This part is green—and also quite toxic. That's because a potato doesn't want to be eaten by a random passerby, so it defends itself. It produces a lot of solanine, a chemical that's really bitter and also poisonous, in the part that's sticking out. That's why it's better to throw away green bits of potato, as they can make you sick.

Beans

Who'd have thought plants would put up such a fight? Beans can be poisonous, too, when they're raw. If someone eats them by mistake, they can expect to get sick. It's best to soak beans for a long time and then cook them for at least half an hour to make sure the toxins are gone.

Why are some plants poisonous?

So that no one will eat them, of course. But people got the better of nature when they learned to cook food because lots of poisons break down at high temperatures and stop working. The interesting thing is that some insects take advantage of poisonous plants. For example, monarch butterfly caterpillars eat poisonous leaves so the caterpillars themselves become poisonous. This stops predators from eating them.

Potato and disinfectant

You will need:

- a glass
- a potato
- peroxide disinfectant
- a knife
- a spoon

Chop up a piece of potato and put it in the glass. Add a tablespoon of peroxide disinfectant and watch what happens. The mixture should start to bubble. The potato contains catalase, an enzyme that can dispose of hydrogen peroxide by breaking it down into two harmless substances: water and oxygen. The bubbles that form on the potato with the peroxide come from the oxygen being produced.

8 THE PORCH

Balloons, a cake, sparklers, and fireworks . . . The party on the porch is in full swing! How come balloons float? Why do sparklers give off sparks? And how come fireworks are all the colors of the rainbow?

GASES

I'm looking forward to getting out into the fresh air.

That's nothing. I'm heading straight into space!

helium

nitrogen

Careful with that tangerine!

Where do balloons go?

One day you've got a nice, big balloon, and the next day it's a tiny, shriveled-up thing—and not because it wasn't tied properly. It's because balloons are made of rubber. Rubber has tiny holes in it that air can escape through unnoticed—and not only air. Helium particles are even smaller than air molecules and pass through the rubber more easily, so a balloon filled with helium will deflate even faster.

GASES

Balloons!

Balloons float beautifully in the air—if you fill them with helium. This gas is lighter than air, so a balloon filled with it will float upward. Just be careful it doesn't fly away! Helium is so light that it can easily escape from Earth's atmosphere into space—as if there wasn't enough of it there already! Helium makes up about a quarter of the mass of the universe.

MATERIALS

What are sparklers made of?

POWDER FROM COAL
Coal is sometimes used for heating in stoves because it burns for a long time. A sparkler contains ground coal so that it will burn well.

OXIDIZER
The more oxygen, the more fire! Sparklers contain oxidizers, substances that have lots of oxygen in them. When the sparkler is lit, oxygen is released from the oxidizer and the fire burns much better.

ALUMINUM AND IRON
Aluminum powder and iron filings are what put the spark in sparklers! These metals catch fire in the burning sparkler and make beautiful sparks.

STARCH
Starch is the glue that sticks all the ingredients in a sparkler together. You can find starch in foods like potatoes.

A dissolving balloon

You will need:
- **tangerine or orange peel**
- **a balloon**

First, blow up the balloon. Then squeeze the tangerine or orange peel so its juice squirts onto the balloon.

The balloon will pop. How is that possible? The juice from the peel contains limonene, which can dissolve the rubber the balloon is made of. The spot where the rubber dissolves opens up, and the balloon pops.

What's hidden inside a firework?

How do fireworks fly into the sky?

You don't just see fireworks—you hear them too. The thing that explodes inside them and sends them flying up into the sky is gunpowder. It's not a new invention—the Chinese have been using it since the 7th century! And the recipe hasn't changed much. It's still made up of coal and sulfur, which burn well, and an oxidizer, which creates oxygen. It makes gunpowder burn so fast that it literally blows up!

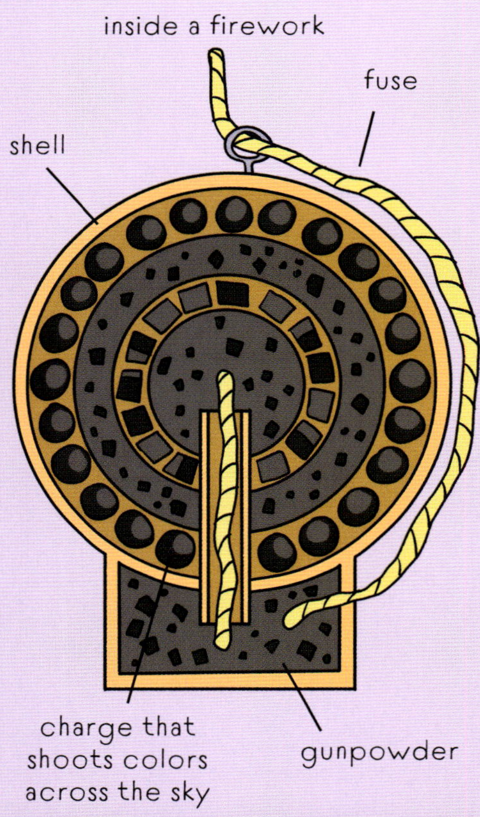

What a show, what a mess

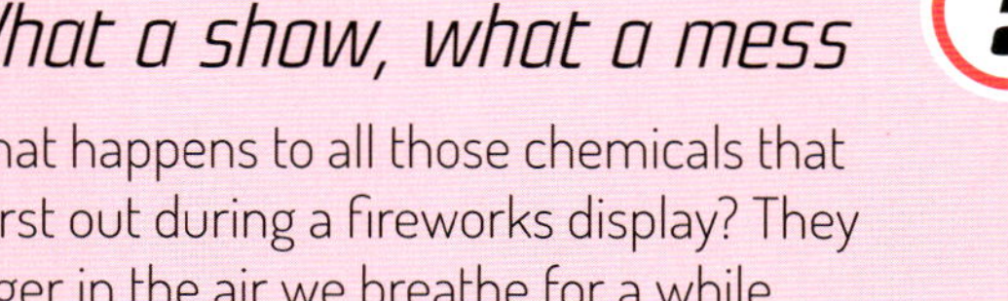

What happens to all those chemicals that burst out during a fireworks display? They linger in the air we breathe for a while and then end up in the water and the soil. Needless to say, this cocktail of chemicals doesn't make animals or plants very happy. . . .

The colors of fireworks

Where do the beautiful colors in fireworks come from? You just need to add in different chemical elements! When they burn, they make fireworks really colorful. Specific elements always produce the same color, but that color may be a surprise. For example, orange copper burns blue!

PURPLE – POTASSIUM
Potassium in fertilizers is fed to plants to make them grow well.

CARMINE RED – LITHIUM
You come across lithium a lot, perhaps without even knowing it. It's used to make batteries for cell phones, tablets, and electric cars.

ORANGE – CALCIUM
Did you know that you yourself are about 2% calcium? Your teeth and bones are full of it. If your body lacked calcium, your teeth would start to decay and your bones would break more easily.

RED – STRONTIUM
Do you know what strontium does in your body? Absolutely nothing! It's there by mistake. It's so similar to calcium that when you eat strontium, your body gets them mixed up. It thinks, "Oh, there's some nice calcium," and then stores the strontium with the calcium in your bones.

YELLOW – SODIUM
If sodium loves any other element, it's chlorine. That's because together they form salt, which makes food taste better.

GREEN – BARIUM
Just about everyone has barium at home, and they probably don't even know it! If you look at the wall, you'll see lots of it. That's because it's commonly used in wall paint.

BLUE – COPPER
Copper is used to make all kinds of things: gutters, coins, roofs, pipes, electrical wires, pots and pans... But why is it so popular? It's not just because of its lovely copper color. It's also tough and doesn't cost a fortune.

WHITE – MAGNESIUM
Magnesium is everywhere—it travels around in cars, airplanes, and submarines. Wherever there's a need for some lightweight metal, there's usually plenty of magnesium.

lithium
calcium
strontium
potassium
barium
copper
magnesium
sodium
I see copper!
I see socium!
I see...
fireworks.

9 THE WORKSHOP

Do you need to fix a bike, put up a shelf, or make a lamp? A workshop will help you with all that and more. From screwdrivers to wood planks, you'll find lots of tools you can use to get the job done!

MATERIALS

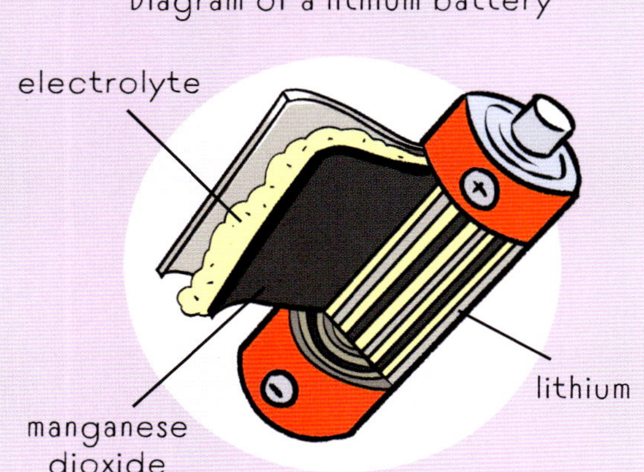

Batteries all around us

Everywhere you look, there are batteries: in your cell phone, the TV remote control, the car. . . . This book might be the only thing that doesn't run on batteries. On top of that, all these batteries are different. The ordinary pencil battery you find in a remote control is very light and small, as it's made of thin layers of lithium metal and a chemical called manganese dioxide. Between them, there's absorbent cotton soaked in electrolyte, a liquid that's good at conducting electricity. There's just one drawback to this kind of battery: it can't be recharged.

PRODUCTION

How to make a diamond

Diamonds—they're beautiful, shiny, expensive, and surrounded by many myths and legends. But how is it possible that carbon, which people regularly burn as coal for heating, can form diamonds? The key is high temperature and some serious pressure. However, that doesn't mean that if you hit burning coal with a hammer, it'll turn into a diamond. You'd need a lot more pressure than that—in fact, over 1,000 times more than you could manage with a hammer. Luckily, people can produce that kind of pressure using machines, and almost anyone can buy a synthetic diamond—for example, in the drill bit for a drill.

A spaghetti printer

A printer can only print using ink on paper, right? Wrong! 3D printers can print using plastic, and you can make just about anything with them. They mostly use long, plastic spaghetti called filament. This is heated up by the printer until it melts. Then all you have to do is apply it somewhere, let it cool and harden, repeat this about a thousand times, and your model of a gecko is complete. However, 3D printers don't just have to use boring old plastic; there are some that can print using metal or concrete. On one you can print an artificial knee and on the other a whole house!

Red-hot batteries

It would be a pain if we had to change the batteries in our phones every day. That's why rechargeable ones are so handy—but they need care, like a pet. Leaving your phone battery completely dead or plugged in too long can cause damage. It might just lose power faster, or it could swell up. That's because chemical reactions inside the battery start making gases like oxygen and carbon dioxide. In rare cases, a swollen battery can even catch fire. To stay safe, unplug your device once it's charged and avoid letting the battery run out completely. Treat your battery well, and it'll keep working like a charm!

Let's conduct!

How are all those parts and wires connected in your cell phone, fridge, or cheese knife? Glue wouldn't work because it doesn't conduct electricity. You need solder: a mixture of tin, copper, silver, and other metals that will melt at a low temperature and join all the parts together properly and conductively. As well as metals, there's one other special component: pine. You won't find any branches or needles, but solder contains a little pine resin, which acts as an acid and gobbles up dirt wherever you're soldering, so the solder sticks better.

Let's shed some light on . . . light

The granddaddy of electric lights

You don't see many incandescent light bulbs these days. But why is that? To find out, we first need to understand how a light bulb works. If you look at a light bulb, you'll see it has two important parts: the glass bulb and the tiny filament inside. The filament is a twisted tungsten wire. Of all the metals, tungsten is the one that can withstand the highest temperature before it melts. And that's exactly what we want! The filament in a bulb glows because it's really, really hot. And the more heat it can withstand, the more it can glow. After all, this is what our sun does too: it shines because it's incredibly hot. But that's also the problem. A light bulb produces more heat than light from electricity. And does it have to have that glass bulb? Well, if it didn't, the tungsten filament would heat up in the air and only glow for a few seconds before burning out. That's because there's oxygen in the air, and oxygen helps things burn. It wouldn't be very practical to change the filament every few seconds. That's why there's a glass bulb to protect it. There's no oxygen inside the bulb, only the gases nitrogen and argon. The filament can't burn in these gases, so the light bulb keeps glowing for several months.

Metals at 4532°F *

* the metals would glow orange at these temperatures

Long, narrow, and bright

Fluorescent tubes shine on you every day, whether you're at school, at home in the kitchen, or on the train. They're long, white, and mysterious because you can't see what's going on inside.

Fluorescent tubes shine because of mercury, which is a very poisonous metal. Luckily, there's not much of it in fluorescent lights, and it's enclosed in a glass tube, so you don't have to worry. But if that breaks, you'd best get away and leave a window open to clear the air.

LEDs are brilliant

You'll find LEDs in your cell-phone screen, the ceiling light, Christmas lights—in fact, just about everywhere. They can be really tiny and are always made from special materials called semiconductors. These only need a little bit of electricity to produce lots of light! And they can do it a lot better than light bulbs and fluorescent tubes. There are lots of semiconductors, the most common being silicon, which is used to make chips for cell phones and computers. If you make an LED from it, it'll glow blue. The color depends on the type of material used for the LED. There are even some made from diamonds! They glow with that ultraviolet light we can't see, so there's not much to look at.

LEDs have another advantage over light bulbs and fluorescent lights: they don't have to be hot. In fact, we don't want them to be. We need to keep LEDs cool so they'll shine brightly for a long time, because a hot LED has a short life. And no one wants to keep buying new lights.

So this must be what it feels like to be a Christmas tree!

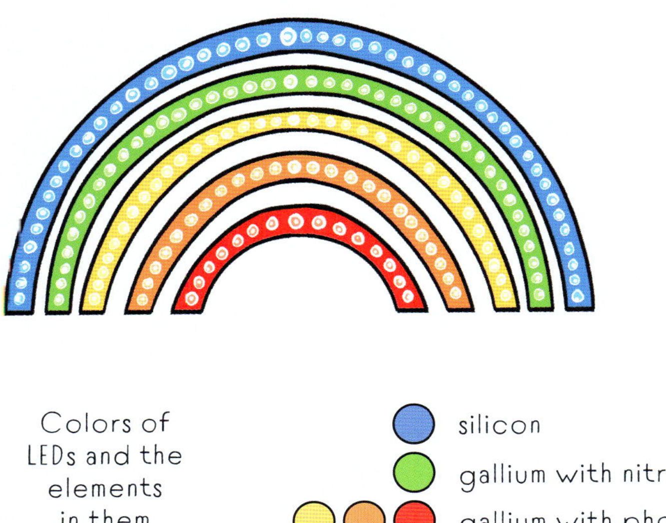

Mercury is found as a gas in a fluorescent tube. You see, even metals can evaporate, just like water. And if electricity gets to work on mercury, it starts to glow—but not with the lovely white light you normally see. It mainly shines with an ultraviolet light. Our eyes can't see that type of light. But if you were a bee, you'd be able to see it. Ultraviolet light can kill cells and bacteria, and you can also find it in sunlight, which allows you to get a tan. But too much ultraviolet light can be dangerous and burn you.

Luckily, fluorescent tubes don't shine this dangerous light on us. That's because there's a white coating called luminophore on them. This takes the ultraviolet light and turns it into the safe bright white light that fluorescent tubes give off.

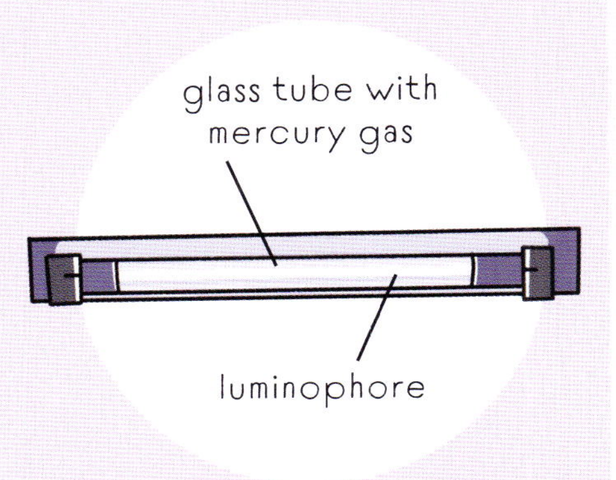

10 THE GARAGE

The garage is home to lots of things, but its main occupant is the car. It needs to be vacuumed and washed before you can head off on a trip!

MATERIALS

A comfortable interior

The first cars that took to the roads 150 years ago may not have had doors, a roof, or lights, but they did have comfy leather seats. Modern cars are full of pleasant materials, most of them synthetic. When the first cars were made, these materials hadn't been invented yet. Now we can produce synthetic vegan leather, which is made from polyurethane instead of animals. This is the same material that's used to make mattresses and sponges.

A tin can full of tin cans

MATERIALS

A passenger car is basically two tons of steel on wheels. Steel is a really solid metal, but it's awfully heavy. What if you wanted a fast racing car that would take off like a rocket? It would definitely help if the car were lighter. A lighter car's body could be made from aluminum and magnesium. Aluminum is also used to make cans. So does that mean a car is a tin can as well?

Magical hydrogen

Electric cars don't always have to be charged from a socket. Some seem to perform miracles. Fill them up with hydrogen and—abracadabra!—they start moving, leaving behind nothing but clean water. But how do they do it? Well, they have something inside them called a "fuel cell." This is a battery made of hydrogen and oxygen, which is taken from the air. Hydrogen and oxygen combine to form harmless water, electricity is produced, and the car can drive off. Pure magic!

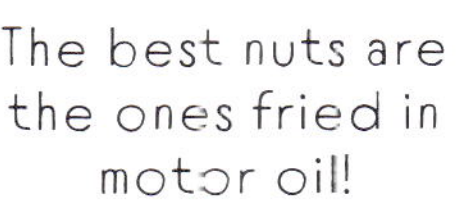

A slippery helper

For an engine to work properly, it needs to be well greased with motor oil. Just to be clear, this is not the kind of oil you find in a kitchen. This stuff's made from petroleum and is very similar to diesel. If you were to fry food in it, in the best case scenario it would give you diarrhea. Similar oils are used as laxatives.

A private car wash

All it takes is a bit of rain and there's mud everywhere. It doesn't matter if it gets on our shoes, but the car windshield is a different story. The wipers alone can't always cope with that kind of dirt; they need a chemical helper: windshield wiper fluid. It contains mainly water and alcohol to keep the glass clean and streak-free. Sometimes there's also smelly ammonia in it, though. It's like a chemical gecko that eats all the flies off the glass.

What's hiding under the hood?

A cushion that can save your life

If a car hits something, the vehicle should protect its passengers as much as possible. To do this, it uses an airbag, which inflates really quickly during a crash and turns into a big, blown-up balloon. But how is this instant cushion created? Upon impact, a chemical explodes inside the airbag and turns into a bunch of nitrogen gas. This inflates the whole airbag so fast you don't even have time to blink.

A mobile power station

No car can run without a battery. And the small, lightweight one from your cell phone certainly wouldn't do the job. It wouldn't even be enough to make the engine sputter. A car has a really big battery. Inside it you'll find lots of the heavy metal lead that's cut up into wide, thin sheets like sliced cheese. These are dipped in a horrible, corrosive substance, sulfuric acid, and they react with it, creating lots of electricity in the process so the engine can start easily. Once the car has started and the engine is revving up, it can generate its own electricity. It even recharges the battery along the way!

A rotten cocktail

Millions of years ago, the ocean was a busy place. There were big fish, algae, and giant plants everywhere. A lot of living organisms also leads to a lot of dead organisms. And there was a big pile of them on the seabed. It wasn't long before this pile began to rot, like food left out of the fridge. The weight of the top of the pile pressed down on the bottom, and chemicals from the bodies of the organisms began to break down into smaller and smaller ones with the help of heat and high pressure. And so, over the course of a few million years, this gave rise to a black cocktail filled with many different molecules: oil.

All the molecules in oil have something in common: they're made of carbon and hydrogen atoms. Some of the molecules are tiny, while others are big and long; some look like chains, while others are twisted and joined together to form rings. To make something out of this mixture, people first have to thoroughly sort through them. The smaller molecules are used to make things like gasoline or headache pills. And the big ones are used to make plastics, tires, and asphalt.

Why do cars have bad breath?

What does a car belch out of its exhaust pipe? Within the dark smoke that appears, there's a whole cloud of chemicals. If it's carbon dioxide or water vapor, it doesn't bother us much. But chemicals that combine nitrogen and oxygen are a different matter. These can be toxic troublemakers that damage people's lungs. And there's one more problem: unfortunately, what comes out of non-electric cars harms our entire planet, worsening the climate crisis. As these chemicals get into the air, they trap the heat from the Sun, and the Earth gradually gets warmer and warmer, making it harder for all plants and animals—including us—to survive.

Gasoline vs diesel

Just like us, cars need to eat. A ham sandwich isn't to their taste; they'd rather have fuel. Different cars like different kinds of fuel, which is why there's more than one kind at a gas station. Most of the time, it'll be gas or diesel. But what's the difference? They're both made from oil and look like chains of carbon atoms with hydrogen atoms around them. Gasoline chains are shorter, and diesel chains are longer. That doesn't mean one fuel is better than the other, but each one is better at something. Gas cars tend to be quicker and faster. That's why sports cars and racing cars run on it—and maybe your family car too. A bus or a truck will be happier with diesel. They need to haul containers full of cabbage or a big load of toys. And a diesel engine is designed to do just that. But the most important thing is not to fill up with the wrong fuel. Otherwise, you won't get very far, and the family trip will end up at a repair shop instead of in the mountains.

GLOSSARY

Atoms and molecules

The whole world is like a giant construction set! And the individual building blocks are atoms. When several of them join together, they form a molecule. Together, atoms and molecules are called chemicals. And they make up absolutely everything: a table, a person, and a flower are just piles of molecules next to each other.

Reactions

When atoms and molecules start to join together, break apart, or rearrange themselves, we call these chemical reactions. They produce different chemicals from what was originally there. Chemical reactions include a candle burning, a person breathing, or fizzy tablets dissolving in water.

Temperature

We feel hot at higher temperatures and cold at lower temperatures. Atoms and molecules are also aware of temperature. The higher the temperature, the faster atoms wiggle and move about. This means chemical reactions also happen more quickly at higher temperatures.

The human body

Life is really just a lot of complex reactions. We eat chemicals such as sugar or fat, enzymes help us to digest them, and in the end we produce a lot of other chemicals. Everything that goes on inside us is because of atoms and molecules and their reactions.

Microorganisms

If we look at the world through a microscope, we discover that there's much more life around us than our eyes can see. Bacteria, molds, yeasts: these microorganisms live in our skin, in our beds, and in our guts. They often carry out lots of interesting reactions and produce weird chemicals.

Materials

Everything is just atoms and molecules put together in some way. But which ones go together? How do you turn them into a sturdy chair, a powerful tool, or a bright light? Chemistry is the study of various raw materials and chemicals that can be used to make things.

Nature

Chemicals are responsible for the smell of cut grass and the taste of strawberries. Nature is full of chemicals, whether they're in honey, rocks, or wood from a tree.

Gases

Matter can be solid like ice, liquid like water, or gas like steam. Air, the helium in balloons, and bubbles escaping from soda are gases we come across every day. They are light, usually invisible, and some are very flammable.

Food

You see a cake; chemistry sees sugars, baking soda, proteins, and fats. Food is a cocktail of chemicals our body has to process to get energy from. People need a lot of them—as well as water, minerals, and vitamins.

Production

It begins with a pile of sand and ends with beautiful glass. In between, there are lots of chemicals. We need to know what raw materials to use, how much to heat things up, and what actually happened in the process. And chemistry can help us with all of that.

FURTHER READING:

Green, Dan and Simon Basher. *Basher Science: Chemistry: Getting a Big Reaction.* Illustrated by Simon Basher. Reprint edition. USA: New York, NY: Kingfisher, 2025.

Biberdorf, Dr. Kate. *Kate the Chemist: The Big Book of Experiments.* USA: New York, NY: Philomel Books, 2020.

Chad, Jon. *Science Comics: The Periodic Table of Elements: Understanding the Building Blocks of Everything.* USA: New York, NY: First Second, 2023.

Heinecke, Liz Lee. *Chemistry for Kids: Home Science Experiments and Activities Inspired by Awesome Chemists, Past and Present.* USA: Beverly, MA: Quarry Books, 2020.

Older Readers

Kean, Sam. *The Disappearing Spoon: And Other True Tales of Rivalry, Adventure, and the History of the World from the Periodic Table of Elements.* USA: New York, NY: Little, Brown and Company, 2018.

Rae, Rowena. *Chemical World: Science in Our Daily Lives.* Canada: Victoria, BC: Orca Book Publishers, 2020.

ABOUT THE CREATORS

Lenka & Jiří

There were once two inquisitive children who were interested in how the world around them worked. They observed anthills, studied the ingredients of shampoo, and watched planes in the sky. And the older they got, the more fascinated they became by one science: chemistry. And that was what brought these two people together. Jiří and Lenka got to know each other when they started studying chemistry in college. Soon they began to share their passion for the natural sciences with the world. After graduating, they threw themselves into popularizing science with the Amazing Theatre of Physics and Chemistry, which allowed them to demonstrate experiments and pass on their enthusiasm and knowledge. When they're not doing magic with experiments, they're organizing science camps, traveling, or writing books.

Tomáš

Tomáš is a male member of the Hominidae family who as a child mastered simple tools, such as pencil and paper, for the transmission and storage of information. In the course of his development, this male kept abreast of advances in technology as he learned to use complicated digital technologies for his purposes. His artistic accompaniments to many products have become the main source of subsistence for his whole tribe

5. května 1746/22, Prague 4, Czech Republic
Authors: Lenka Karpíšková and Jiří Vlach
Illustrator: © Tomáš Koepcký, 2024
Editor: Tom Velčovský
Translators: Graeme and Suzanne Dibble
Proofreader: Scott Alexander Jones
Graphics and typesetting: Roman Havlice

Printed in China by Leo Paper Group.

www.albatrosbooks.com

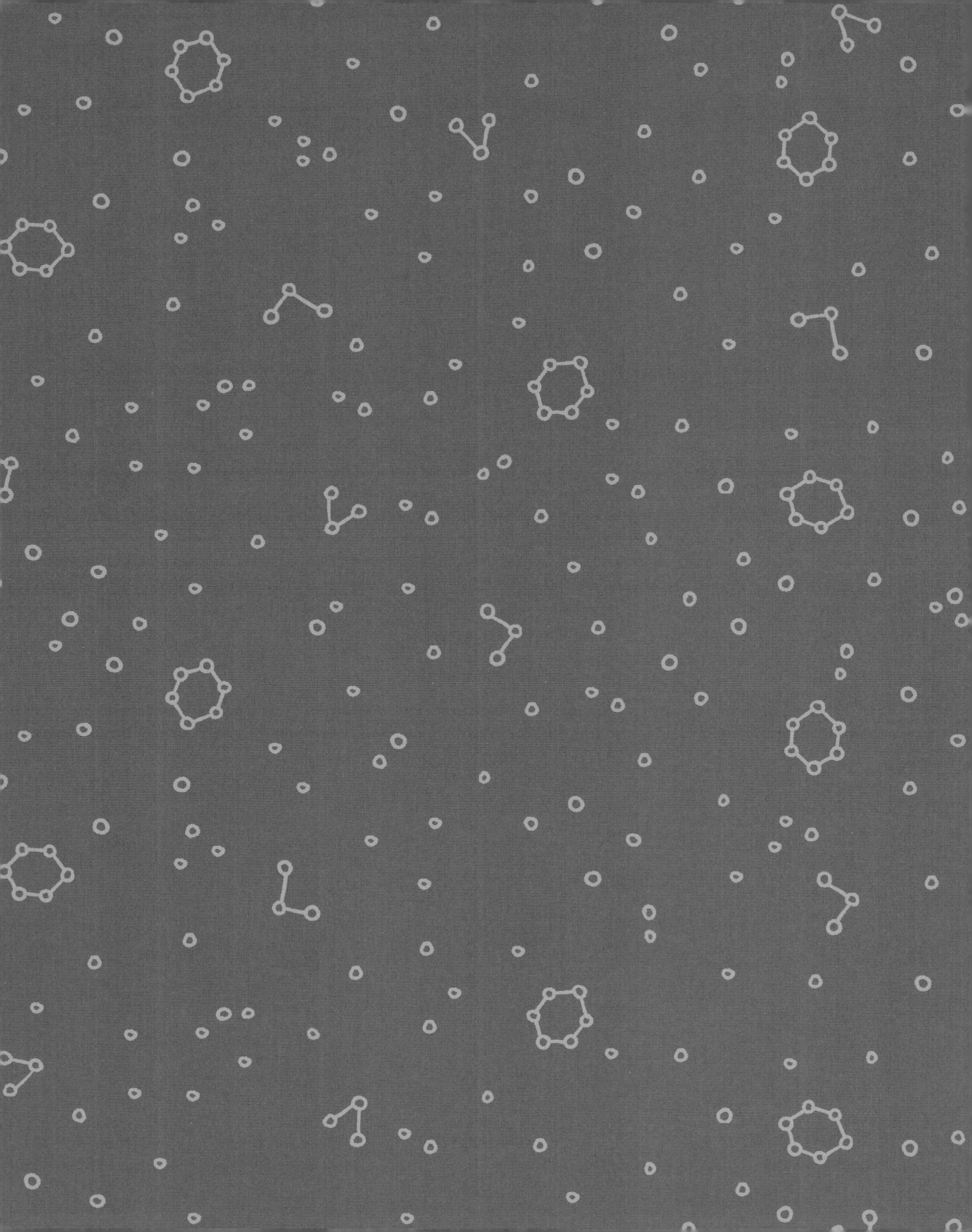